SPOTLIGHT ON POETRY

WHAT KIND OF POEM? 3

Contents

Collected by Brian Moses and David Orme

COLLINS

Acknowledgements

Whilst every effort has been made to contact the copyright-holders and to secure the necessary permission to reprint these selections, this has not proved to be possible in every case. The publishers would appreciate any information which would allow them to do so.

'Good Company' by Leonard Clark, reprinted by permission of the literary executor of Leonard Clark; 'Dear Spider' by Angela Topping; 'Ice Dawn' by Patricia Leighton; 'Bank Holiday Diary' by Janis Priestley; 'Kenning My Dad' by Angela Topping; extract from 'Pen Rhythm' by Benjamin Zephaniah; 'Oil Tanka' by Cedric Sponge; 'Croc City' by Brian Moses, © Brian Moses, first published in *Croc City* (Victoria Press, 1993). Reproduced by permission of the author; '1349 Cinquain', '1415 Cinquain' by Dave Calder; Prayer 'February Night' by Fred Sedgwick; 'Elegy for Grandad' by John Kitching; 'Huff' by Wendy Cope; 'What am I?' by Judith Nicholls; 'Dare' by Margaret Blount; 'Titanic' by Andrea Lewis.

Published by Collins Educational
An imprint of HarperCollins*Publishers*
77–85 Fulham Palace Road
Hammersmith
London W6 8JB

www.**fire**and**water**.com

© HarperCollins*Publishers* 1999

First published 1999

Reprinted 0 9 8 7 6 5 4 3 2

ISBN 0 00 310 346 3

Designed by Clare Truscott
Cover Design by Clare Truscott and Kate Roberts
Illustrations by Tim Archbold, Rob Chapman, Abigail Conway, Tamsin Cook, Emma Garner, Brett Hudson, Patricia Linnane, Paul McCaffrey, Melanie Mansfield, Katty McMurray, Ben Morris, Zara Slattery, Holly Swain, Brian Walker

Printed and bound in Scotland by Scotprint

Collins Educational would like to thank the following teachers and consultants who contributed to the research of this series:

Maria Artoon (Barnfield School); Mrs J. Bibby (St Paul's C of E Primary); Jenny Cox (Melcombe Primary School); Jason Darley, Liz Hooley (Jessop Primary School); Mrs M.G. Farnell (High Meadow First School); Ann Hughes; Karina Law; Alison Lewis; Louise Lochner, Gateway Primary School; Chris Lutrario; Lesley Moores (Princess Royal Primary School); Hannah O'Gorman (St Edward's Primary School); Sally Prendergrast (Brooke Hill School); Jenny Ransom; Betty Root; Sheila Stamp and Michael Webster (Castle Lower School); Shri Toplek, Westminster City School; Jill Walkinton; Sue Webb; Jill Wells (St Andrews C of E Primary School).

Good Company

I sleep in a room at the top of the house
With a flea, and a fly, and a soft-scratching mouse,
And a spider that hangs by a thread from the ceiling,
Who gives me each day such a curious feeling
When I watch him at work on the beautiful weave
Of his web that's so fine I can hardly believe
It won't all end up in such terrible tangles,
For he sways as he weaves, and spins as he dangles.
I cannot get up to that spider, I know,
And I hope he won't get down to me here below,
And yet when I wake in the chill morning air
I'd miss him if he were not still swinging there,
For I have in a my room such good company,
There's him, and the mouse, and the fly, and the flea.

Leonard Clark

Two Limericks

There was a young lady from Gloucester
Whose parents both thought they had lost her.
From the fridge came a sound
And at last she was found.
The problem was how to defrost her.

Anon

A flea and a fly in a flue
Were imprisoned, so what could they do?
"Let us flee," said the fly.
"Let us fly," said the flea.
So they flew through a flaw in the flue.

Traditional

Dear Spider

Thanks for the invitation
to your cosy dinner for two.
I'd really love to come
but I can't think what to do.
I can't decide just what to wear
my clothes are all so fine
and I'm not certain where to find
a suitable sort of wine.
I'm not used to dining out,
it's really not my thing.
I tend to snatch meals
when I am on the wing.
My mealtime conversation
is limited in kind.
In short I feel that
I really should decline.
It's not that I don't like you
but we are so far apart;
I can't see it working out
although you want my heart.

Yours sincerely
Fly

Angela Topping

Ice Dawn

The garden is refrigerated, frosted,
zipped tight into a strait jacket of white;
the helpless arms of tall trees are ghost-misted
and frozen waterdrops catch the thin light.
The lawn below is spread with lethal needles
of granulated grass stems, captured leaves,
and wandering paw prints make small icy puddles
between the border plants, like halted thieves.

Slowly the hoar mist lifts and edges sharpen,
low in the sky a lemon sun pulsates,
teases the dawn's tight fist and fingers open;
frost crystals turn opaque, the garden waits.
Wise, it has seen too many winters to worry.
Silently life beats on beneath the ice.

Patricia Leighton

Bank Holiday Diary

Friday

We caught the train today at six.
Everyone was packed in so tightly
we felt like a packet of Weetabix.
We were off for a short holiday
at Seaside-over-Sand-in-the-Sticks.

Saturday

The sun shone on our heads all day
making us feel like melted ice cream.
We even felt too hot to play,
lolling around like runny jelly,
wobbling and then dribbling away.

Sunday

Today it rained so we stayed in,
bored as planks on a pirate ship.
We threw the packed lunch in the bin
after Dad sat on it all morning.
'Well,' said Mum. 'What a way to keep thin!'

Monday

It hailed frozen-drops of hard rain
as big as coloured gobstoppers.
We packed up all our things again.
Then packed, like canned sardines,
we came home on a crowded train.

Tuesday

School!

Janis Priestly

Kenning My Dad

He comes home smelling of outside
A bootstamping coat remover.
When he sits at the table
He's a food exterminator
A coffee-consuming pudding praiser.
He's a mountain strider, birdwatcher,
A cheering on at rugby shouter.
A dolls house maker, breadbaker,
Cooking pasta in the kitchen on Sunday.
He's a vegetable nurturer
Digging in the garden in the rain
A leekbringer, soup inventor.
At work he's a computer tapper
Brainworker, travelling on a train worker.
At home he's our dad –
a bighugging loudlaughing funloving
Daft teasing dad with a prickly face.

Angela Topping

From Pen Rhythm

The rhythm of the pen goes bubbling
dancing round the page.
no disease can't cripple it
can't die of old age,
the rhythm of the pen goes to and fro
high and low where you can't go
the rhythm of the pen will not stop now
pen rhythm is in full rage.

The rhythm of the pen goes ring ding dong
left and right and can't go wrong
the pen plans the rhythm and the rhythm sings the song
the strain is on the rhythm but the rhythm well strong,
the rhythm of the pen goes here and there
always with harmony always with care
the rhythm is full still there is some spare
pen rhythm get wild pen rhythm don't fear.

Benjamin Zephaniah

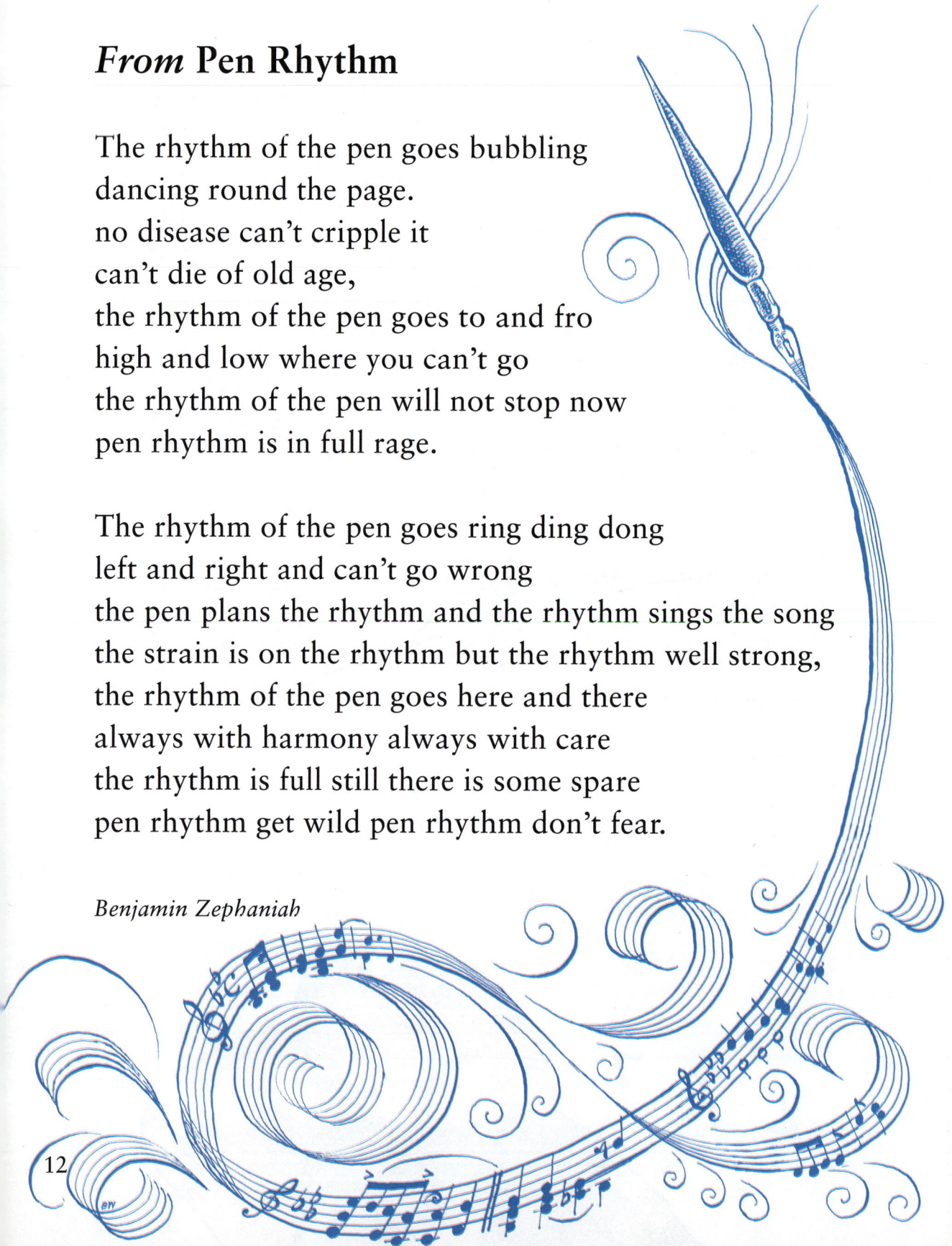

Oil Tanka

I come from darkness
sucked through giants' drinking straws.
Given refinement,
I burn to air in engines,
die with rainbows in wet streets.

Cedric Sponge

Croc City Rap

Beneath the streets of New York
    there are sewers that stretch for miles,
they say that the sewers of New York
    are filled with crocodiles,
and alligators that frightened folk
    have just flushed down the pan,
when the creatures stopped being babies
    and started snapping at their hands.

Chorus:

Croc city,
down below when the city sleeps,
croc city,
snapping away to a hip hop beat
croc city.

Pity the poor sewer walker
     taking his nightly stroll,
thinking about hot coffee
     at the end of his dark patrol.
Then out of the slime, a snapper
     raises it's ugly head,
how fast you can sprint down a sewer pipe
     when a crocodile wants you dead...

Chorus:

Croc city,
down below when the city sleeps,
croc city,
snapping away to a hip hop beat
croc city.

The State department issues advice
    to those who find a croc,
whatever you do don't go after it,
    don't chase it with a rock.
Don't start thinking you're Dundee
    out to catch a snapper.
If he opens his mouth, then you can be sure
    this croc, he ain't no rapper!

Croc city,
down below when the city sleeps,
croc city,
snapping away to a hip hop beat
croc city.

Croc city,
down below when the city sleeps,
croc city,
snapping away to a hip hop beat
croc city.

Croc city, croc city, croc city,
croc city, croc city,
CROCK CITY... YEAH!

Brian Moses

Cinquain Prayer, February Night

On this
cold night I kneel
with thanks for catkins, pale
green under the lamplight by the
roadside.

Fred Sedgwick

1349 Cinquain

Rats, fleas,
boils and black spots:
Death scythes through the country,
no walls are strong enough to stop
disease.

1415 Cinquain

Arrows
darken the sky.
As if maddened by flies
the horses throw their armoured knights
to die.

David Calder

Elegy For Grandad

There's a photo of my Grandad
On the wall in the hall.
He's a tiny man with a white moustache.
In his wrinkled hand there's a thin cigarette
Which is dripping grey, sinister ash.

I was five, I think, when we first met.
It was the last time too.
And yet
I have to say
I remember him clearly still today.
More than sixty long, long years away.

The memory of how he kindly played with me,
Although he was then so slowly dying,
Has firmly stayed with me.
He was the gentlest of men.
I fear I shall not see his like again.

John Kitching

Sea Lions

The satin sea lions
Nudge each other
Toward the edge
Of the pool until
They fall like
Soft boulders
Into the water,
Sink down, slide
In swift circles,
Twist together
And apart, rise again
snorting, climb
Up slapping
Their flippers on
The wet cement:
Someone said
That in all the zoo
Only the sea lions
Seem happy.

Valerie Worth

Huff

I am in a tremendous huff –
Really, really bad.
It isn't any ordinary huff –
It's one of the best I've had.

I plan to keep it up for a month
Or maybe for a year
And you needn't think you can make me smile
Or talk to you. No fear.

I can do without you and her and them –
Too late to make amends.
I'll think deep thoughts on my own for a while,
Then find some better friends.

And they'll be wise and kind and good
And bright enough to see
That they should behave with proper respect
Towards somebody like me.

I do like being in a huff –
Cold fury is so heady.
I've been like this for half an hour
And it's cheered me up already.

Perhaps I'll give them another chance,
Now I'm feeling stronger
But they'd better watch out – my next big huff
Could last much, much, much longer.

Wendy Cope

Write a Poem

"Write a poem" our teacher said
"A poem about an animal or a place,
Something that happened to you
In the holidays.
Better still write about yourself.
What you feel like,
What's inside you
And wants to come out."

Stephen straightaway
Began to write slowly
And went on and on
Without looking up.

John sighed and looked far away
Then suddenly snatched up his pen
And was scribbling.

Ann tossed back her long hair
And smiled as she began.

But I sat still.

I thought of fighting cats
With chewed ears
And dogs sniffing their way along
Windy streets strewn with paper
But there seemed nothing new
To say about them…
The holidays? Nothing much happened.
And what's inside me?
Only the numbness of cold fingers.
The grey of the sky today.

John sighed again.
Peter coughed.
Papers rustled.
Pens scratched.
A blowfly was fuzzing
　　　　　At a window pane.
　　　　　　　The tittering clock
　　　　　　　　Kept snatching the minutes away.

　　　　　　I had nothing to say.

Olive Dove

What am I?

I am light as a breeze,
a puff of pink smoke;
a chin-sticker, lip-gripper,
fluffy pink joke!

I cling to your fingers,
I curl round your thumb;
then like a small duvet
I wrap round your tongue.

Judith Nicholls

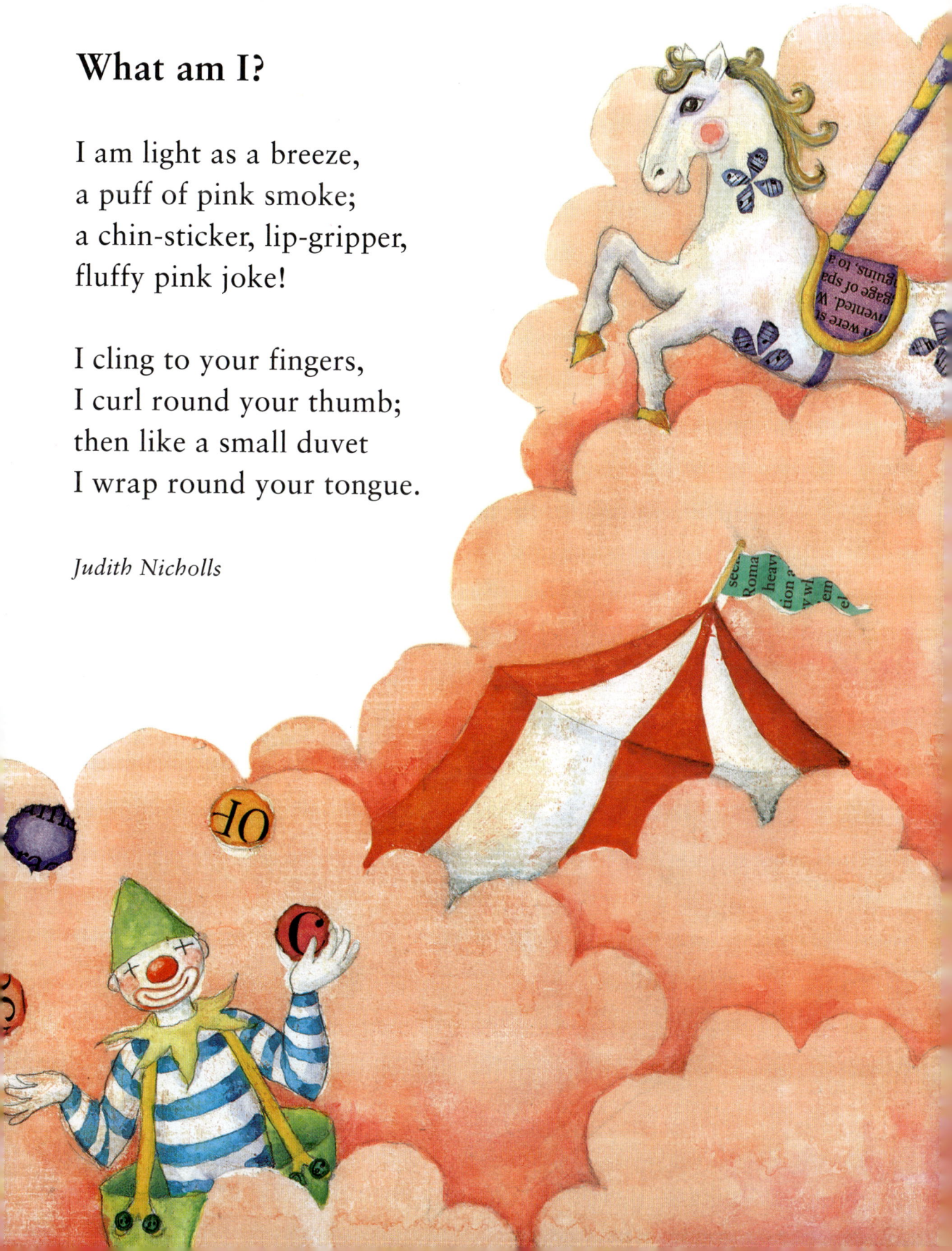

The Titanic

Beyond the wildest waves
and below the raging sea
sunk deep in the dark deep gloom
the guts of the Titanic
lie spilled on the ocean floor

lost in a battle of the swirls and swells
this mighty ship is stilled
its torn and twisted steel
wedged deep in the murky slime
as if crushed by a giant's fist

silent black shadows lurk
around ghostly open windows
a treasure trove of debris slips
into the shifting shape of the ocean sand
softly sighing in its watery grave

the massive hull stands proud and alone
rusticles dangling over portholes
like eyelashes with tears
the echoes of voices crying from the deep
are lost in the bubbling white surf

Andrea Lewis

Dare

"I dare you to
I bet you daren't"

"Course I dare"

"Go on then"

"I don't have to"

"You daren't do it"

"I dare. I just don't want to"

"You're chicken"

"I am not"

"Yes you are"

"I'm braver than you"

"No you're not"

"Yes I am"

"Why?"

"Because I can say 'NO'"

Margaret Blount

Glossary

Dear Spider
decline   say no

Two Limericks
flue   part of a chimney

Ice Dawn
refrigerated   as cold as in a refrigerator (fridge)
strait jacket   a jacket with special straps to stop the person wearing it from moving
lethal   deadly
granulated   covered in powdery crystals
hoar   frost
pulsates   throbs
opaque   lets light through but can't be seen through

Kenning My Dad
exterminator   destroyer
nurturer
a person who helps something grow

***From* Pen Rhythm**
cripple   injure
harmony   notes of music sounding together

Oil Tanka
refinement making pure

Cinquain Prayer, February Night
catkins   hanging flowers of the willow tree

1349 Cinquain
scythes   cuts like a scythe (a sharp tool used for cutting plants)

Sea Lions
satin   a shiny material

Huff
make amends
do something to show that you are sorry

Write a Poem
blowfly   large type of fly

Titanic
debris   broken-up remains
rusticles   hanging 'icicles' of rust

Index of poems by title

Index of poems by first line